NO Problem!

· · · · · · · · · · · · ·

AN EASY GUIDE
TO GETTING
WHAT YOU
WANT

NO Problem!

AN EASY GUIDE
TO GETTING WHAT YOU WANT

BY **KEN WATANABE**

ILLUSTRATED BY **ELWOOD H. SMITH** • ADAPTED BY **SARAH L. THOMSON**

Viking

An Imprint of Penguin Group (USA) Inc.

Viking

Published by Penguin Group

Penguin Young Readers Group, 345 Hudson Street, New York, New York 10014, U.S.A.

Penguin Group (Canada), 90 Eglinton Avenue East, Suite 700, Toronto, Ontario, Canada M4P 2Y3
(a division of Pearson Penguin Canada Inc.)

Penguin Books Ltd, 80 Strand, London WC2R 0RL, England

Penguin Ireland, 25 St Stephen's Green, Dublin 2, Ireland (a division of Penguin Books Ltd)

Penguin Group (Australia), 250 Camberwell Road, Camberwell, Victoria 3124, Australia
(a division of Pearson Australia Group Pty Ltd)

Penguin Books India Pvt Ltd, 11 Community Centre, Panchsheel Park, New Delhi – 110 017, India

Penguin Group (NZ), 67 Apollo Drive, Rosedale, North Shore 0632, New Zealand
(a division of Pearson New Zealand Ltd.)

Penguin Books (South Africa) (Pty) Ltd, 24 Sturdee Avenue, Rosebank, Johannesburg 2196, South Africa

Penguin Books Ltd, Registered Offices: 80 Strand, London WC2R 0RL, England

First published in the U.S.A. in another form in 2009 by Portfolio, a member of Penguin Group (USA) Inc.
This edition first published in 2010 by Viking, a division of Penguin Young Readers Group

1   3   5   7   9   10   8   6   4   2

Text copyright © Kensuke Watanabe, 2007, 2009, 2010
Illustrations copyright © Elwood H. Smith, 2010
All rights reserved
Originally published in Japanese by Diamond Inc., Tokyo

LIBRARY OF CONGRESS CATALOGING-IN-PUBLICATION DATA
Thomson, Sarah L.
No problem : an easy guide to getting what you want / by Kensuke Watanabe ; illustrated by Elwood H. Smith ;
adapted by Sarah L. Thomson.
p. cm.
Adaptation of: Problem solving 101 / Ken Watanabe. c2009.
ISBN 978-0-670-01203-9 (hardcover)—ISBN 978-0-670-01254-1 (pbk.) 1. Problem solving—Juvenile literature. I. Smith, Elwood
H., 1941- II. Watanabe, Ken. Problem solving 101. III. Title.
BF449.T46 2010
153.4'3—dc22
2009037075

Manufactured in China   Set in Century Expanded   Book design by Nancy Brennan

Contents

Why Problem Solving?

Problem-Solving Kid Basics

Case #1:
Rock Bands and Root Causes

NO Problem!

AN EASY GUIDE
TO GETTING
WHAT YOU
WANT

Why Problem Solving?
. . . .

EVERYONE HAS TO make decisions.

You might be an A student, a soccer star, a drummer in a band, or a future millionaire. You might be all of these things at once. But whoever you are, you have to make decisions.

The decisions you make depend on what you're trying to do—pass math class, win a game, save the environment. No matter what you're trying to accomplish, you have to set goals, face challenges, and try to overcome them. Every single day.

There's a basic approach to solving the problems you face. If you use it, it can lead you to satisfying solutions. But chances are, nobody ever bothered to show it to you.

One of my reasons for writing this book was to show everybody a simple way to solve problems. But I wasn't merely trying to teach a bunch of skills. Being a problem-solver isn't just an ability—it's a whole mindset, one that lets people bring out the best in themselves and change the world around them in a positive way. Instead of just accepting the way things are, real problem-solvers try to make a difference. Imagine what the world would be like if Mahatma Gandhi, Martin Luther King Jr., Eleanor Roosevelt, John F. Kennedy, or Steve Jobs had thought that they couldn't change anything.

First, I hope this book helps you tackle the problems in your own life. And then you might come to see that bigger dreams and accomplishments are also within your reach.

Problem-Solving Kid Basics

KIDS FACE SOME pretty tough challenges—the kinds of things that might cause most people to throw up their hands and give up. But problem-solving kids don't give up.

Maybe you think that to be a problem-solving kid you have to have a special talent or a lot of luck. But the truth is that these kids are just like you—except they've learned how to think, make decisions, and take action on their own. They *act* instead of *reacting* to what other people do. And they've also picked up some helpful problem-solving tools along the way.

Problem-Solving Kids—and Others

First let's talk about what problem-solving kids are *not*. There are several common attitudes that can get in the way of real problem solving. Maybe you know people at school or home who have these kinds of attitudes. Maybe (just maybe) you have a few yourself.

Sofie Sigh

Sofie Sigh is the kind of person who gives up the minute she meets a challenge. She just sighs and says, "I'll never be able to do that."

Maybe she *could* do something if she tried. Sometimes she has a great idea or notices a problem that could be fixed, but she's terrified of failing and having people laugh at her. So instead of speaking up or taking action, she sits around feeling sorry for herself.

Sofie Sigh doesn't take control of her own life. She's sure that nobody understands her. Whenever anything goes wrong, it's always somebody else's fault.

She often says things like:

▶ "I'd better not try. What if I can't do it? Everybody will laugh at me!"

▶ "It's my parents' fault. It's the school's fault. It's your fault!"

▶ "Nobody understands me. Nobody cares about me. Everybody picks on me."

Chris Critic

Chris Critic is never afraid to speak up. Whatever the plan, he's right there, ready to point out problems and shoot down everybody's ideas. If anyone tries something and fails, he's the first to say, "I told you so!" And he's always ready to blame somebody else when things go wrong.

Chris Critic has a lot to say about other people's mistakes. But he never does much of anything himself. And as you probably know, being a critic is easy; getting stuff done is the real challenge. Even if you know the right way to do something, it isn't much use unless you roll up your sleeves and get to work.

Chris Critic might not understand that his criticism won't get the job done. Or maybe he's afraid to try something himself.

Chris Critic usually sounds like this:

▶ "Well, that definitely won't work. What a stupid idea!"

▶ "I told you that would get screwed up. It's all your fault."

▶ "Come on. Why can't you get it done?"

Darla Dreamer

Darla Dreamer may be more fun to hang around with than Chris Critic, but she's got her head in the clouds. She loves coming up with new ideas, but she never bothers to think about how to turn her dreams into real plans. And she definitely doesn't try to get anything done. For her, it's more fun thinking about things than actually doing them.

Here's what Darla Dreamer says to herself:

- "Someday I'm going to write a novel!"
- "Wouldn't it be great to start my own business?"
- "I want to be a doctor when I grow up."
- "I'm an idea person. Don't bother me with all those details!"

Gary Go-Getter

When you first meet Gary Go-Getter, he doesn't seem like a non–problem-solver at all. He doesn't sit around worrying or criticizing. He loves to jump into action, especially when something goes wrong.

Gary Go-Getter knows how to take action—that's good. He's not afraid of problems or hard work—that's even better. But if he took a moment to stop and think before rushing into action, he'd be able to achieve so much more.

He thinks that most problems happen because somebody didn't try hard enough. He never stops to think about *what* he's trying to do, or if there's a better way to get it done. He's not interested in understanding why he's having problems—just in trying harder and harder to fix them.

Here's what Gary Go-Getter sounds like:

▷ "I'll never give up. I'll get it done!"
▷ "I know this will work if I just try a little harder."
▷ "Thinking about a problem is a waste of time. It's what you do that matters!"

Are you one of these types? Do you ever find yourself sighing and giving up? Do you find it easier to criticize other people than to try something yourself? Do you love to dream but hate to plan? Do you attack problems head on, but forget to put on the brakes when you're not getting anywhere?

Or are you more like a problem-solving kid?

Problem-solving kids set goals. They get things accomplished. Like Gary Go-Getter, they don't sit around and agonize over problems. But unlike him, they think about what's *causing* the problems. They make plans before they take action. And they're willing to change those plans if a new challenge comes up, or if the plan doesn't work. They learn from what goes wrong and from what works well.

Problem-solving kids have a positive attitude. They don't worry too much about what they can't control—instead, they figure out what they *can* change. First they look for the real cause of a problem. Then they make a plan and put it in motion. And as soon as they've tried to fix a problem, they check to see how well the solution worked and if it could work any better.

Once they find a balance between thinking and acting, problem-solving kids can accomplish amazing things.

Here's what a problem-solving kid says:

▶ "Okay! I'm going to get this done in three months."

▶ "This is a problem. But I'm not going to sit around worrying. I'm going to figure out what I can do to fix it."

▶ "So what really made this happen?"

▶ "To fix this, we're going to need to do X, Y, and Z. Let's get started!"

▶ "How did that idea work? What went wrong? Is there something we could do better next time?"

The important thing to know about problem solving is that it's not a talent that some people have and others don't. It's a habit that anyone can learn. By developing the right skills and the right attitude, you can become a problem-solving kid.

What Is Problem Solving?

Problem solving can be broken down into a four-step process.

1) Understand what's going on.

2) Figure out the real cause of the problem.

3) Come up with a plan that will work.

4) Put that plan into action until the problem is solved, making changes as you need to.

These steps are a package. It doesn't do any good to figure out what's causing a problem if you don't take action. It doesn't do any good to take action if you don't know the right action to take. You've got to complete all four steps to solve a problem.

It sounds simple, right? The catch is, a lot of the time, we don't do what seems simple and obvious.

Take Carlos, for example. Carlos's math grades have been slipping. Maybe he thinks, "I've got to get better grades," and then hopes it will happen, even though he doesn't take any action. His math grades will probably stay right where they are, because he didn't figure out what's causing the problem or what he can do about it.

Or maybe Carlos declares, "I'm going to quit the soccer team so that I've got more time to study." But what if his problem wasn't the *time* he spent studying, but the *way* he was studying? Then even if he does something that drastic, his grades won't get better. He will have given up playing soccer for nothing.

If Carlos is a problem-solving kid, what does he do instead?

1) He tries to understand what's going on. He checks his grades on tests for the last few months. "This is a real problem," he thinks, looking at the grades going down—down—down.

2) Carlos tries to figure out exactly what's causing the problem. "What am I getting wrong on the tests?" he asks. He might break up his tests into categories: algebra, fractions, and geometry. Then he checks to see which categories he's getting wrong. To his surprise, he discovers that his score in algebra is actually going up a little! His score in fractions is staying the

same. It's only the geometry score that's been falling.

Carlos doesn't stop there. He creates subcategories for geometry, including area, angles, and volume. He looks over his tests again to see exactly where he's having trouble. Pretty soon he knows just what the problem is. He doesn't understand trapezoids and cylinders.

3) Now Carlos has to come up with a plan. He could wake up thirty minutes earlier each day, and spend the time going over these types of geometry problems. Or he could set aside thirty minutes before he goes to sleep and do the same thing. Or he could try to study not more but better. He could get help from a teacher or a friend, or ask his parents to hire a tutor. After thinking about it, Carlos decides to ask his friend Ryan—who he knows aced the last math test—for help.

4) Finally Carlos puts his plan into action. Then he checks out his grades on the next test to see if they've gotten better. If they haven't, he goes back to his plan to figure out what went wrong and how to fix it.

Problem solving isn't complicated. You just have to follow those four steps: understand the situation, identify the specific problem, make a plan, and put the plan into action. Even issues that seem huge and complicated at first can be tackled, especially if you break them down into smaller, more manageable problems and deal with them one by one.

Once you learn the basic approach to problem solving, you can stop panicking when things go wrong. You'll be confident that you'll be able to solve any problem you face—whether it's about grades, home, or friends.

Problem-Solving Toolbox: Logic Tree

A logic tree is a great tool to use when you solve problems. It will help you identify the possible cause of your problem and come up with lots of potential solutions.

The key to making a logic tree is to break a problem down into categories. You want to be sure you don't leave anything out, and that you group similar categories on the same branch of the tree.

For example, if you wanted to break your class into categories, you could do it in all sorts of ways. You might want to do it by gender:

boys and girls. You could do it by height: kids taller than four feet and kids four feet and shorter. Or you could divide the class into kids who are right-handed, left-handed, or ambidextrous (able to use either hand).

The logic trees for these breakdowns would look like this:

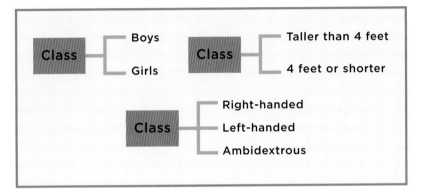

Pretty simple, right? Notice that no one is left out—every kid in the class falls into one of these categories. And none of the categories overlaps another.

You could also break your class down according to the clubs students belong to. To build this tree, put the biggest, most general groups on the left: "Belongs to a school club" or "Does not belong to a school club." (Remember that nobody should be left out. Everyone in the class has to go into one of these two groups. Sometimes you may need to add a category called "Others" to make sure you have a place to put everyone.) As you move to the right, your categories get more and more specific. "Art," "Games," and "Sports," for example. Then you can break each category down further, until no more divisions are possible.

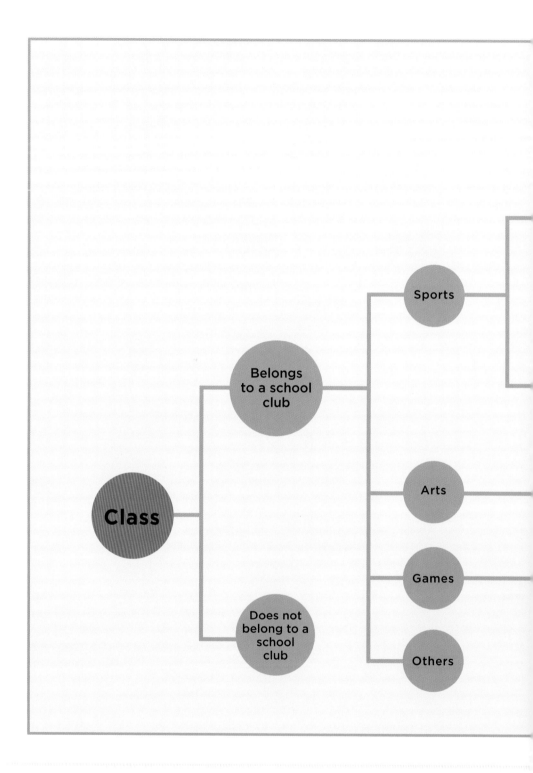

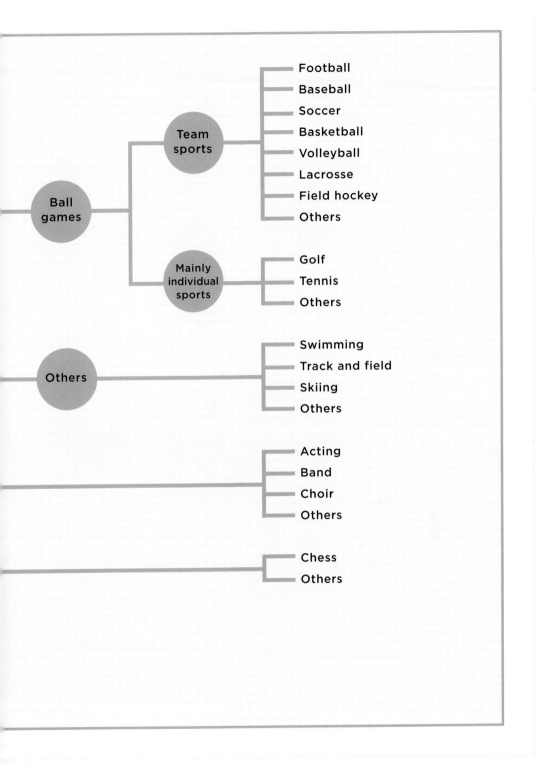

Using a different kind of logic tree can help you analyze problems. For instance, here is a logic tree for the question: How can you increase the amount of pepper that comes out of a pepper shaker without changing how quickly or how hard you shake it?

A logic tree will help you come up with lots of different ideas.

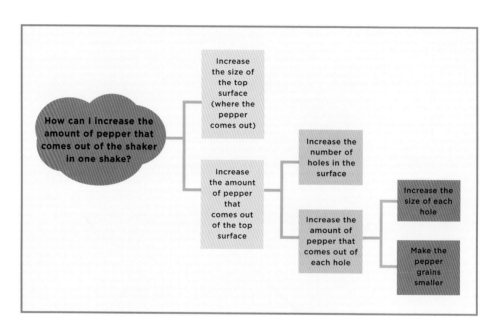

To build this tree, you start with the problem on the left: "How can I increase the amount of pepper that comes out of the shaker in one shake?" Two solutions you can think of are to increase the size of the surface where the pepper comes out or to increase the amount of pepper that comes out of the surface area that's already there. So you make two branches. You can think of two ways to get more pepper to come out of the top of the shaker, so you add two branches to that option: increase the number of holes in the shaker, or make it so more pepper comes out of each hole. You add two more branches to that last option: either make the holes bigger or make the pepper grains smaller. Your logic tree has given you four possible solutions.

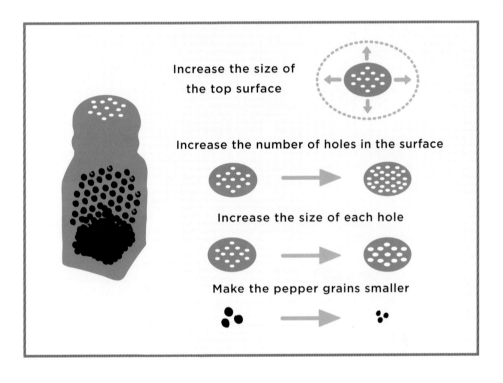

Case #1

Rock Bands and Root Causes

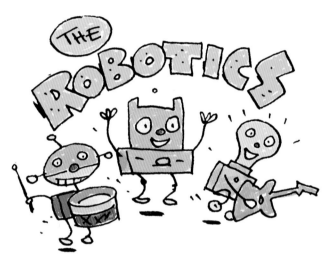

LIFE IS FULL of challenges. Every day you run into obstacles that might keep you from reaching your goals. But that doesn't mean you should give up.

Instead, step back and try to figure out what's making the problem happen. What's the actual root cause of the problem?

For example, think about what happens when you go to the doctor if you're sick. First the doctor asks you some questions about what's wrong. Then she might take your temperature, run some tests, or take an X-ray. She's collecting information and analyzing it to figure out what's making you feel bad—the root cause of your illness. Only after she's figured out exactly what's wrong does the doctor prescribe something: medicine for a cold or a cast for a broken bone.

Note the differences between a symptom (for instance a headache), a root cause (fever), and a prescription (take cold medicine). The better you get at understanding symptoms and figuring out root causes of problems, the better you'll get at creating good solutions.

Here's how this process works in problem solving.

Step 1: Find the root cause of the problem.

    1A: List all the possible causes of the problem that you can think of.

    1B: Develop a hypothesis—a theory that you can test. Your hypothesis will take the possible causes you've thought of and use them to explain what you think might be happening.

    1C: Figure out how you can test your hypothesis. What information do you need? How can you get it?

    1D: Use your information to identify the root cause. Compare your hypothesis with the information you have gathered. You may need to change your hypothesis in light of what you have discovered. When everything fits together, you have your root cause.

Step 2: Develop the solution.

    2A: List a lot of different solutions that might solve the problem.

    2B: Figure out what actions are most likely to help. Which ones do you want to try right away, and which can wait until a little later?

Step 3: Make a plan to put your solution into action.

RITA

Let's see how this process works for a struggling young rock band called the Robotics.

It all started when Rita got home from a rock concert. The first thing she did was call her best friends, Remi and Rad. "Hey, we're going to start a band tomorrow!" she announced. "I'll sing. Remi, you play guitar. Rad, you're the drummer. We'll meet right after school and start practicing! All right?"

"Wait a second," said Remi.

"Hold on," said Rad.

But Rita had already hung up. Remi and Rad sighed. "Here we go again," Rad said. They do love Rita, though, so they wanted to help make her dream come true.

Remi borrowed her brother's guitar and started teaching herself how to play. Rad didn't have a drum, so he used a cardboard box. At first Rita's singing was so bad that both Remi and Rad had to wear earplugs.

But slowly things improved. Remi learned more and more chords. Rad saved up enough for a real drum. And Rita's voice got better and better.

One day, Rita, Remi, and Rad were walking home from school when Rita announced, "We're going to put on a concert at the gym on Saturday! In fact, we're going to do one every month from now on! All right?"

"Saturday? That's impossible!" Remi exclaimed.

"The school won't let us use the gym," Rad said.

Rita hates hearing things like "That's impossible!" or "Nobody's ever done that." She was determined. "What's wrong with you guys?" she yelled. "We're trying to become a professional band, right? How are we going to get started if

we never play in front of a crowd? I'm going to ask the principal about using the gym. You guys start letting people know about the concerts."

To her friends' surprise, the principal agreed to let the band use the gym each month. Remi and Rad each told people

about the concert, and there was actually an audience at the Robotics' first show.

But three months later, Rita was fuming again. "We only had ten people at the first show, and fifteen at the two after that," she grumbled. "Aren't you guys telling people about our concerts? Why can't we get that gym full?"

Remi and Rad promised to figure out the root cause of the problem and how to fix it.

Step 1: Find the root cause of the problem.

1A: List all the possible causes of the problem that you can think of.

The problem is that very few people are coming to the Robotics' concerts. Possible causes:

1) People don't know about the concerts.

2) People don't want to (or can't) go to the concerts.

3) People went to one concert, but then they stopped coming.

Once you've come up with a lot of possibilities, there are several ways you can organize them to help you look at the problem. You can make a logic tree:

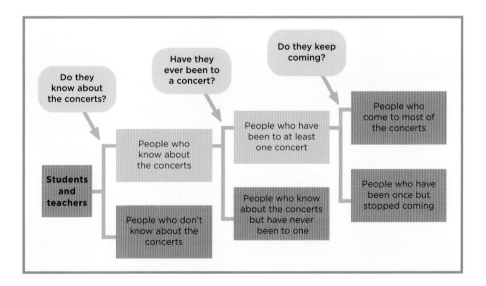

Or you can try a similar tool: a yes/no tree.

Problem-Solving Toolbox: Yes/No Tree

You can use a yes/no tree to help you figure out a problem's root cause. A yes/no tree divides people or things into groups based on the answers to yes/no questions. At every stage you can either put a group into a "bucket" of things that are all the same or divide the group further by asking another yes/no question. After each question, everything must fall into one of the buckets—no exceptions. By seeing how many fall into each bucket, you can see more easily where the real problem is.

Here's a yes/no tree for the band's problem. It asks the same three questions as the logic tree did:

▶ Do people know about the concerts?

▶ Have they ever been to a concert?

▶ Do they keep coming?

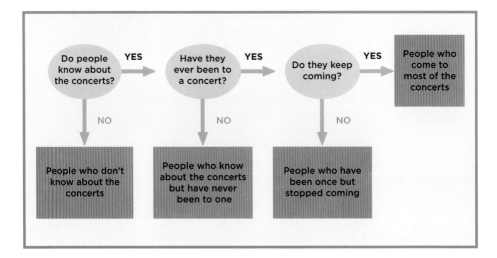

1B: Develop a hypothesis.

A hypothesis is like a hunch. It describes what you think is probably going on that is causing the problem, but you haven't proved it yet.

Remi and Rad have to come up with a hypothesis to explain why people aren't coming to their concerts, so they take a second look at their yes/no tree. To make the tree more helpful, Remi and Rad ask some *why* questions.

- ▶ Why don't people know about the concerts?
- ▶ If they know about them, why aren't they coming?
- ▶ If they've been to a concert, why don't they come back?

These questions will help with figuring out the likely root cause of their problem.

This time, when they look at the yes/no tree they try to figure out how big the group in each bucket is. If one bucket has an especially large number of people in it, that may show them where the problem lies.

There are about 500 teachers and students in the school, and each of them has to go in one of the buckets. How many people knew there was a concert going on, and how many people didn't? They admit that they didn't try very hard to get the word out. Rad says, "We only told a couple of the kids who sit next to us. And Rita probably didn't invite anybody, because even though

she's bossy, she's really pretty shy." So they figure that only about 25 people actually heard about the concert. This means 475 people fall into the bucket of people who didn't know about the concert.

Rad estimates that about 15 of the kids who knew about the concerts showed up for at least one. That's based on an estimate that about 60 percent of the kids in their school like rock music. Rad assumes that anyone who likes rock music would want to come to a free rock concert. And he and Remi think the same people have been showing up at each concert. So they figure that all of the people who went to one concert came back for the others.

They plug these numbers into their yes/no chart. Now it looks like this:

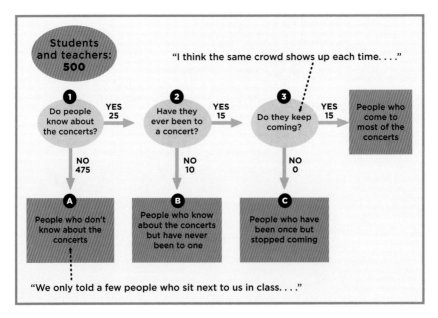

If their numbers are right, then the cause of their problem is a lack of awareness. Out of the 500 people in the school, 475 don't even know that the concerts are going on.

1C: Figure out how you can test your hypothesis.

To test their hypothesis, Remi and Rad have to do some research. They need to figure out how many people actually fall into each bucket, not just how many they guess go in each.

It would take forever to ask each of the 500 people in school individually. So they write a three-question survey:

1) Raise your hand if you know about the Robotics' concerts.

2) If you know about the concerts, raise your hand if you've been to one.

3) If you've been to a concert, raise your hand if you're attending them regularly.

Remi and Rad ask each homeroom teacher to read the questions out loud and count how many people raise their hands. This will be quick and easy. It shouldn't take the teachers more than three minutes to ask the questions.

1D: Use your information to identify the root cause.

Here's what Remi and Rad found out from their survey.

1. Did you know about the Robotics' concerts?

Yes = 150 people

No = 350 people

2. If you know about the Robotics' concerts, have you ever been to one?

    Yes = 20 people

    No = 130 people

3. If you've been to a Robotics' concert, did you attend more than once?

    Yes = 15 people

    No = 5 people

With all this information, Remi and Rad are able to figure out the real breakdown of people in each bucket of their yes/no tree.

They had assumed that only 25 people in school knew about their concerts, but in fact, 150 knew. They had also assumed that if people knew about the concerts, around 60 percent of those people would come. But actually only a little over 10 percent of the people who knew about the concerts have come to one. And most of the people who've been to one concert have been to more than one—but not all.

After they have gathered all this information, Remi and Rad realize that it won't do much good just to make sure that more people know about the concerts. They also have to find out why people who know about the concerts don't want to come, and why a few have been to one concert but don't want to come back.

Remi and Rad could try asking every one of the 130 people who knew about the concerts but didn't come *why* they didn't come. But they don't really have time. Instead, they decide to interview five people who didn't come. This should give them a pretty good idea of the main reasons people don't come. They'll also interview people who have been to the concerts, including the five who came to one but didn't come back.

First set of interviews: Why do some people who know about the concert stay away?

Here's what Remi and Rad heard from the people they interviewed:

- ▶ "Yeah, I heard that you're doing a concert every month. But I don't know what kind of music you guys play, and to be honest, I don't know how good you really are. . . ."
- ▶ "I don't know you guys. I heard about your band, but I was like, 'Who are they?'"
- ▶ "Are you kidding me? You guys are a middle-school band. How can you be worth watching on a Saturday?"
- ▶ "I wanted to go, but the concerts are at noon on Saturdays,

right? I have baseball games then. Frank and Mike couldn't go for the same reason."

▶ "I don't even listen to music at home. Why would I go to your concerts?"

Remi and Rad learn that there are three main reasons why people who know about the concert aren't coming.

1) They don't know what kind of music we're playing or how good we are.

2) The show time doesn't work with their schedules.

3) They don't care about music.

"Interesting!" Rad exclaims. "The people who don't care about music are never going to come. But I bet we can do something about the people who don't know our music or who can't come at noon on Saturday afternoon." Remi and Rad talk to some more people about their schedules, and figure out that they'd be able to draw a bigger crowd on Saturday evenings.

Second set of interviews: Why do some people who've been to one concert stop coming?

Here's what Remi and Rad learn from their second interviews:

▶ "I love you guys! You should be a professional band! I'm going to brag to everyone that I was at your first show! Of course, I'm going to every one of your concerts!"

▷ "Rita's husky voice is great. I loved when she sang the ballad. I'll always be there!"

▷ "You guys were great, but the songs were all the same. If you guys keep playing the same songs all the time, the crowd will start getting bored."

▷ "Remi, I loved your guitar solo! There may be months when I can't make the concert, but I want to come as much as possible!"

▷ "Love the music, but it gets boring when you keep playing the same songs the same way over and over. Don't you get bored performing the same songs at every concert?"

Remi and Rad feel great hearing that lots of people enjoy their music. But the really important thing they get from these interviews isn't praise— it's learning that people are bored when they play the same songs over and over. This could be why some people aren't coming back.

Remi and Rad have checked out their first hypothesis—that people aren't coming to the concerts because they don't know about them. And they've found out that it wasn't right. More people know about the concerts than they thought. With the new information they've gathered, they can revise their hypothesis so it matches what they have discovered: A few people aren't showing up because the time doesn't work for their schedules, but most of them don't come because they don't know what kind of music the band plays or if they're any good. And some of the people who did come are getting bored because the Robotics don't play any new songs. Because they made a hypothesis and then gathered the information to check and revise it, Remi and Rad now have a really good idea of the root cause of their problem.

Step 2: Develop the solution.

2A: List a lot of different solutions that might solve the problem.

The main problem seems to be that people don't know what kind of music the band is playing or how good they are. To solve this, the Robotics need to do two things: let more people know about the concerts and make more people want to come. So Remi and Rad create a logic tree to figure out all the methods of communication they could use to get these two things done.

They use the logic tree to help them come up with as many different kinds of ideas as possible. At this stage, they don't say

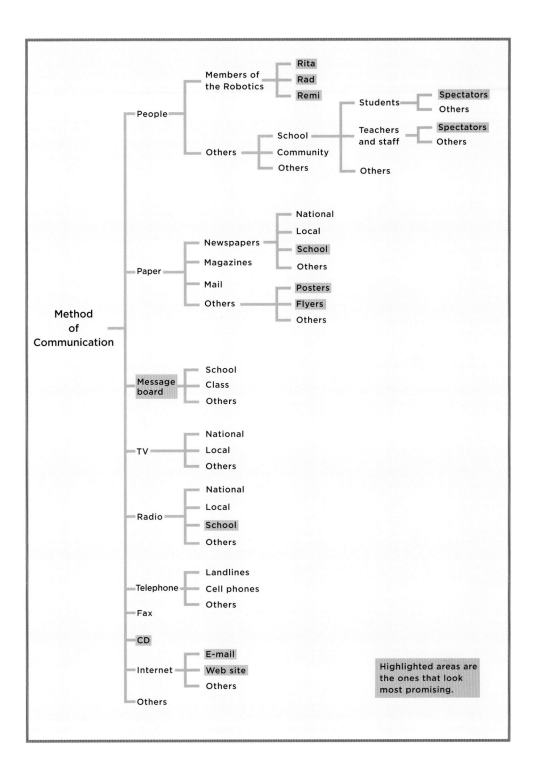

things like, "TV? That's impossible!" or "We can't afford a radio ad!" They know that what seems like a crazy idea might lead to a really useful solution.

Once Remi and Rad have come up with as many ideas as they can think of, they look at the logic tree and highlight the ones that they think would work best. If possible, they want each idea to do two things: raise awareness about the concerts and make people want to come. For example, they can advertise on the school radio station. But just announcing the date, time, and location of the concerts will only raise awareness. However, if they play part of a song, that might make people want to come.

Here's what their list of ideas looks like:

Method of communication	Idea	Makes people aware?	Makes people want to attend?
❶ Members of the Robotics	Perform in each class during homeroom	✓	✓
❷ Spectators	Ask audience to invite friends to the next show	✓	✓
❸ School paper	Get the paper to run interviews with band and fans, and to give details of next show	✓	✓
❹ Posters	Make cool posters and put them up around school	✓	✓
❺ Flyers	Hand out flyers to students and teachers as they leave school	✓	✓
❻ Message board	Put concert details up on each class's message board	✓	
❼ School radio	Ask radio host to play a song and announce the next concert	✓	✓
❽ CDs	Create a CD to hand out to students with a note about the next concert	✓	✓
❾ E-mail	E-mail all students and teachers the concert details	✓	
❿ Web site	Create a Web site with song downloads, band member bios, and event listings for upcoming shows	✓	✓

Now they have ten ideas.

They add three more to their list, to deal with the other problems they found based on information from their interviews.

11) Change the concert starting time to 5:00 p.m.

12) At each concert, sing at least two new songs and switch the song order to keep the music fresh.

13) Have Rad tell jokes and stories about the band between the songs to entertain the crowd.

Now they have thirteen ideas. But can they put them all into place before the next concert? Some of the ideas will take a long time to do right. Others will be expensive. Since Remi and Rad have a short amount of time and not too much money, they'll have to figure out which ideas are really worth doing.

2B: Figure out what actions are most likely to help.

Remi and Rad decide that there are two key questions to ask about each idea: How effective will it be? And how simple is it to do?

To easily compare all the ideas, they create a matrix.

A matrix is a simple chart. It can be a quick way to see which ideas will help you the most.

On one side of the matrix, Remi and Rad rate the impact of their ideas—how much effect each will have—from low to high. Along the bottom, they rate the ideas from hard to easy. Each of their possible solutions gets a spot somewhere on the matrix.

For example, take solution #1: playing a song in each home-room. This should be very effective, because every student in school will hear the Robotics. But it would be hard to do. They'd have to convince the teachers to let them play, and it would be a lot of work to set up all their equipment in each class. So this idea goes in the top left box.

How about solution #6: putting up the concert details on the message board? This won't be very effective. Only a few people look at the message board on any given day. And even if they

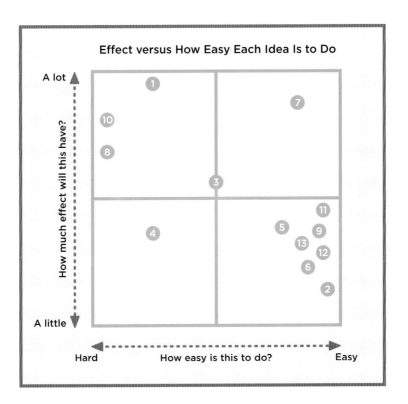

do see the notice, it won't necessarily make them want to come. However, it's pretty easy to do. Remi and Rad put this idea in the lower right box.

When they have all the ideas arranged on the matrix, the best solutions will be in the top right box. Those should be both very effective and easy to do.

Step 3: Make a plan to put your solution into action.

First Rad and Remi tackle the ideas in the upper right corner of their matrix. Then they move on to the ideas in the upper left and lower right boxes. The ideas in the lower left box are the least helpful.

Then Remi and Rad realize something. They've been assuming that they (and Rita) would have to do everything themselves. But what if they got some help?

For example, take idea #4: Make cool posters and put them up around school. None of the Robotics is good at art, so a poster they made wouldn't be very good. That's why they put this idea in the lower left box: hard to do and not very effective. But what if they asked their friend Albert to help? He's great at art. That could move this idea over into the top right box—easy to do and effective.

The same thing is true of ideas #8 and #10: Create a CD and

Create a Web site. They don't know how to do either of these things, so they put those ideas in the upper left box. But if they can find some friends who know how, they could move the ideas over to the upper right box.

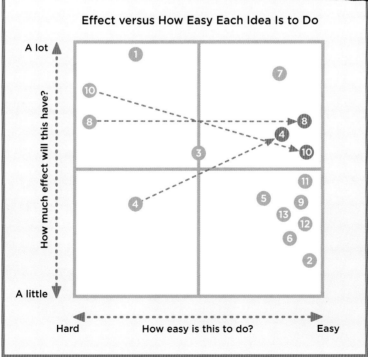

Effect versus How Easy Each Idea Is to Do

How much effect will this have?

A lot

A little

How easy is this to do?

Hard

Easy

With some help and careful planning, Remi, Rad, and Rita manage to accomplish all thirteen ideas.

The Next Robotics Concert

So what happened at the Robotics' next concert?

Two hundred people showed up. The gym was full from wall to wall. Problem solved!

Case #2

Lofty Goals and Solid Achievements

PROBLEM-SOLVING KIDS HAVE big dreams. But they have something else too—plans that break their big dreams down into smaller goals. This helps them get where they want to go. They figure out the best way to meet each goal and keep moving toward the big dream.

Here's how it works:

Step 1: Set a clear goal.

Step 2: Look at the gap between where you want to be (your goal) and where you are now.

Step 3: Create a hypothesis about the best way to close the gap and achieve your goal. To do this:

   3a: List as many ideas as possible.

   3b: Put together the best ideas to create your hypothesis.

Step 4: Check the hypothesis. To do this:

   4a: Figure out what information you need to test the hypothesis and how to get it.

4b: Gather the information and use it to test the hypothesis.

Step 5: If your hypothesis doesn't work out, revise it until it does.

Step 6: Make an action plan.

Let's see how this process works out for Albert. Albert dreams of going to Hollywood someday and becoming an animator. He's great at drawing, but he needs to learn to animate on a computer, and he doesn't own one. What should his plan be?

Step 1: Set a clear goal.

Imagine you're Albert. Write your goal on a piece of paper.

Maybe you wrote down "Buy a computer" or "I want a computer." But these goals won't help Albert very much. Why not? They're too general. They don't state how or when Albert is going to reach his goal, or even exactly what he wants.

Albert will have an easier time reaching his goal if he's very specific: "I want to buy a $500 used Apple computer within six months, without borrowing money from anybody." This goal lays out *what* Albert wants (a used Apple), *when* he wants it (within six months), and *how* he wants to get it (without borrowing money).

Step 2: Look at the gap between where you want to be (your goal) and where you are now.

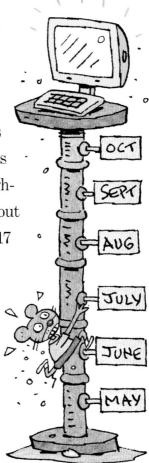

Albert's first step is to figure out exactly how much money he has now and how much he can expect to have in six months.

He has about $150 in savings. He gets an allowance of $20 a month and earns another $12 a month walking his neighbor's dog for $3 an hour. He spends about $15 a month, on average. So he saves $17 a month.

If Albert doesn't change anything about the amount of money he makes or spends he will have $252 in six months. He wants $500. The gap between where he'll be and where he wants to be is $248.

Step 3: Create a hypothesis about the best way to close the gap and achieve your goal.

3a: List as many ideas as possible.

Albert knows that if he changes nothing he won't close the gap. He'll have to come up with some new ideas.

Sometimes it's hard to think of really new ideas—ideas that might change the way we've been doing things. At first, Albert's list looks like this:

▶ Ask Mom to increase allowance.

▶ Save money.

▶ Buy a lottery ticket.

It's not a great list. The first idea doesn't work because Albert wants to do this by himself—no relying on other people. The second idea isn't specific enough. And the third one is pretty much a long shot.

But if Albert uses a logic tree, he might have better luck coming up with a wide variety of ideas.

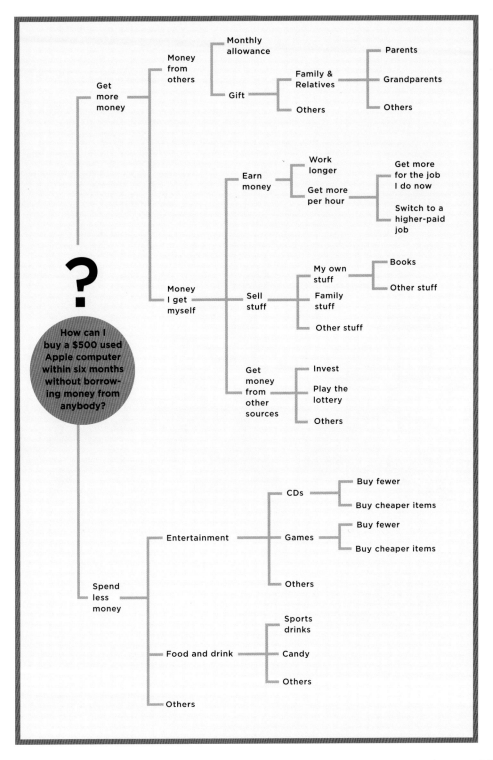

Albert starts out with two ways he can come up with money—by getting more or spending less. Then he fills in each category with all the ideas he can think of. "Are there other ways to solve this problem?" he keeps asking himself. This makes his tree grow vertically, by adding more branches. "Exactly how am I going to do that?" he asks every time he adds a category. This makes his tree grow horizontally, breaking each branch into twigs.

3b: Put together the best ideas to create your hypothesis.

Albert looks at his tree carefully to see if there are any branches he should cut off entirely. He makes notes about which ideas probably won't work.

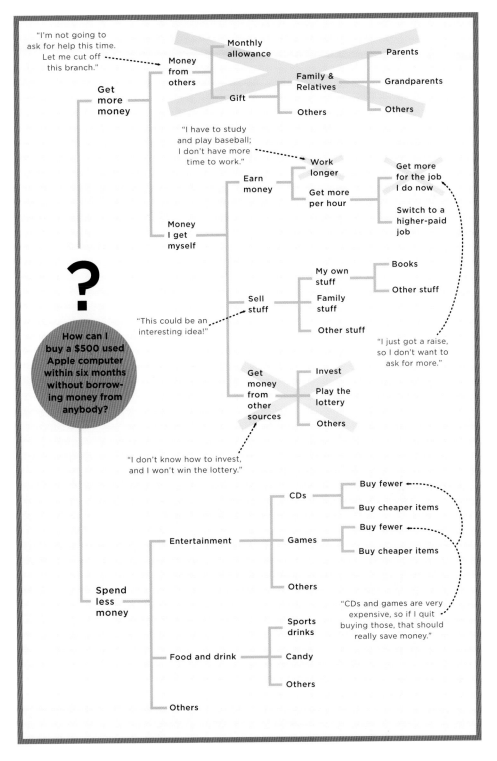

After looking at his tree, Albert comes up with a hypothesis: "I can buy the computer within six months if I switch to a higher-paying job, sell some used books, and stop buying CDs and games." But this is still a hypothesis—not a solution—because Albert doesn't know yet if it's really true.

Step 4: Check the hypothesis.

4a: Figure out what information you need to test the hypothesis and how to get it.

To check his hypothesis, Albert makes a problem-solving chart. For each of his three best ideas (switching to a higher-paying job, selling some of his stuff, and not buying any CDs or games) he notes down his hypothesis, his reason for thinking it's true, the actions he'll take to find out if it's true, and where he's going to get the information.

Issue	Hypothesis	Why I Think So	How I Can Check	Where to Get This Information
1 How much less money can I spend?	I can save lots of money if I quit buying CDs and games.	CDs and games are the most expensive things I buy.	Spending breakdown: check spending for the last three months and see where I can spend less.	Receipts and my memory of what I spent.
2 How much can I make selling stuff?	I can probably only make about $15.	I only have comic books to sell.	Look for stuff to sell and research prices.	My room and the basement; internet used-book sites
3 How much more can I make from a higher-paying job?	I can go from $3 an hour to $8 an hour.	I don't know what Kevin does, but I heard he makes $8 an hour.	Ask five friends what they make. Ask neighbors if they have jobs and what they'd pay.	Interviews with friends and neighbors

Now it's clear what Albert has to do: ·

- ▷ Study his past spending and figure out where to make cuts.
- ▷ Search for stuff he can sell and research prices.
- ▷ Check with his friends to see how much they get paid for their jobs.
- ▷ Ask the neighbors if they have any work available and what they might pay.

4b: Gather the information and use it to test the hypothesis

1: How much less money can Albert spend?

First Albert tries to remember everything he's spent over the last three months. He knows he buys $4 worth of comic books every month and a sports drink after every baseball game. He remembers buying a video game last month, and a CD the month before, and some candy every few weeks. Here's what he comes up with:

1 Month Ago	2 Months Ago	3 Months Ago
Sports drink: $1	Sports drink: $1	Sports drink: $1
Sports drink: $1	Sports drink: $1	Sports drink: $1
Sports drink: $1	Sports drink: $1	Sports drink: $1
Sports drink: $1	Sports drink: $1	Sports drink: $1
Comic books: $4	Comic books: $4	Comic books: $4
Candy: $1	Candy: $1	Candy: $1
Video game: $9	CD: $9	
Total: $18	**Total: $18**	**Total: $9**

Next Albert figures out how much he spends on average each month on each type of purchase. Surprise! His two biggest expenses are sports drinks and comic books—not CDs and games. But Albert doesn't *want* to give up sports drinks—he's really thirsty after baseball! And he'd hate to give up comic books too. His friends all read them, and Albert doesn't want to be left out. He realizes that there are things he's willing to give up and things he's not. To help organize his thoughts about this, he makes a matrix. He write down all the items he buys, with the most expensive ones on the top and least expensive on the bottom. Then he positions them from left to right according to how hard it would be for him to give them up. The easier something would be to give up, the farther right he puts it on the chart.

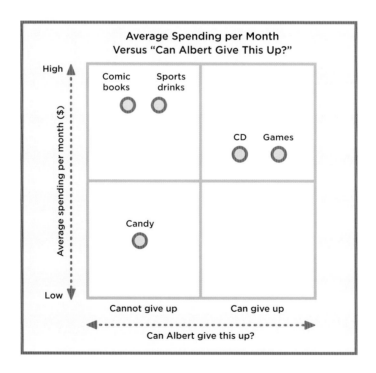

CDs and games fall into the upper right corner of the matrix. They cost a lot and would be fairly easy for Albert to give up. Candy, on the other hand, doesn't cost a lot—and Albert really likes it. There's not much point in giving it up.

But what about sports drinks and comic books? Albert doesn't want to give them up—but they do cost a lot. He decides to think of some creative ways to cut costs. Instead of buying

a sports drink at the store, he can buy a cheaper powdered mix, make it at home, and bring it to the game. Albert can suggest sharing the cost of comic books with a friend. That will save him half of their price, and he'll still get to read them.

Albert makes a chart to see exactly what all these changes will do:

Item	What to do	Average Spending per Month		
		Before	Now	Savings
Sports drinks	Switch to powder; cut spending by 50%	$4	$2	$2
Comic books	Share with friend; cut spending by 50%	$4	$2	$2
CDs	Give up; save 100%	$3	$0	$3
Games	Give up; save 100%	$3	$0	$3
Candy	Continue to buy	$1	$1	$0
Total		**$15**	**$5**	**$10**

Albert can drop his monthly spending from $15 to $5. In six months time, that will increase his savings by $60. But that still leaves him $188 to go.

2: How much can Albert make selling stuff?

Albert searches his room, looking for things to sell. He comes up with a bunch of old comic books and a brand-new diction-ary that he never uses (he'd rather use the dictionary online). He checks out used-book Web sites and figures that he can sell these books for $25.

Next, the basement. Albert finds his dad's old golf bag, and his parents agree that he can try to sell it. The sporting goods store downtown offers him $25 for the golf bag, so with the $25 for the books, Albert is $50 ahead. His gap is down to $138.

3: How much more money can Albert make from a higher-paying job?

Albert starts out by asking five of his friends and their older brothers and sisters what they do for part-time jobs and how much they get paid. Here's what he finds out:

Friend	Job	Pay
Juan	"I'm a babysitter for families in my neighborhood."	$8 an hour
Gen	"I'm bilingual in Japanese and English because I used to live in Japan. I teach Japanese at the community center."	$6 a hour
Javier	"I love dogs, but my parents won't let me have one. My aunt lets me walk hers."	$2 an hour
Kevin	"I designed a Web site for my dad's business and word spread. Now I'm developing a few more."	$8 an hour
Anne	"I walk my neighbor's dog, but he doesn't pay me very much."	$2 an hour

Albert realizes that special skills—like Web site design or speaking two languages—can increase the amount you get paid. Jobs that anybody can do—like walking a dog—don't pay as much. And most of the jobs that pay really well are for older kids.

Next Albert visits his neighbors to ask what kind of work they might need, and how much they'd pay. Here's what they tell him:

Neighbor	Comments
Mr. Wright	"You could walk our dog, but I can't pay that much. How about $3 an hour?"
Mr. Picasso	"Do you want to do our laundry for $2.50 an hour?"
Mrs. Chanel	"Well, you can walk our dog, but I don't know if you can handle her. She's a big dog, and she barks at people and chases other dogs. But I'll pay you $3 an hour."
Mr. King	"You can mow our lawn and rake up the leaves in the fall. How about $3 an hour?"

Step 5: If your hypothesis doesn't work out, revise it until it does.

Albert needs $138 more to reach his goal. To make that in six months, he'll need to make $23 more a month than he's making now. Working four hours a month, that means he needs to earn almost $6 an hour more than he does now—almost $9 an hour. But nobody seems to be offering that kind of money to kids Albert's age, and he doesn't have a special skill that could make his work more valuable. Albert is about to give up on this idea when

he has a brainstorm. What if he walked three dogs at once? If each owner paid him $3 an hour, that would be $9 an hour!

Now there's no gap between where Albert is and his goal. In six months he should have his computer!

Step 6: Make an action plan

Albert is now at the most important step: He has to actually *do* everything he's planned.

Even the best plan in the world won't work if you never put it into action. You need both planning *and* action to meet your goals.

A schedule can help a lot in turning a plan into action. Write down all your steps and when you're going to do each one. Remember to keep track of your progress and change the plan if you need to. Most plans run into some problems at some point. What if one or two of Albert's neighbors decide they don't need him to walk their dogs anymore? If that happens, Albert won't need to panic, because he already knows how to solve problems. He can come up with a new plan to replace the lost income, and put that new plan into action.

Case #3

Soccer School Pros and Cons

PROBLEM-SOLVING KIDS ARE great at making decisions. They usually don't end up regretting the choices they've made, because they took the time beforehand to think about all their options and figure out the best one.

Meet Kiwi. Kiwi has always loved soccer. She's short and tiny, but she's fast, agile, and good. In fact, she's the starting striker for the under-seventeen national team, even though she's only in her first year of high school.

Kiwi just got back from a world tour with her team, and all she can think about is going to Brazil to train. Her team played an exhibition match with the Brazilian Under-17 team—and lost 10–0. The Brazilians were simply better at everything! Kiwi believes that she needs to train and play in a much more competitive environment if she's going to be a world-class player.

As Kiwi traveled, she also realized how much she was learning from spending time in other countries. If she goes to live in Brazil, she'll have a chance to learn another language and live in another culture. She doesn't want to pass that up!

Kiwi's Search Begins

First Kiwi asks her parents if she can transfer to a school in Brazil to play soccer. They know how important soccer is to Kiwi, and they say yes. But they tell her that she'll have to keep her grades up, too, and that she's got to find a school where tuition will be under $3,000 a year.

Kiwi starts researching Brazilian soccer schools on the internet. She finds out right away that every member of Brazil's U-17 soccer team came from one of two schools.

Rio High School's team won last year's high school soccer championship. They have a fancy Web site, accessible not only in Portuguese but also in English, Spanish, Italian, French, and Japanese. They've got a specially designed program for foreign students, and thirty kids from the U.S. already go there. And it's right in Rio de Janeiro; Kiwi can try out surfing at Rio's beaches. She checks the tuition and finds that it's exactly $3,000 a year.

This sounds perfect, but Kiwi does a little more research. She tries to find Amazon High School, which was the runner-up in last year's championship. But she can't find the school's Web site until she tries a search in Portuguese. The site is only in Portuguese, so she uses a dictionary and learns that the school doesn't have any foreign students. And it's about two hours away from Rio. Finally, the tuition is $5,000 a year.

Kiwi makes a pros-and-cons grid to compare the two schools.

Problem-Solving Toolbox: Pros and Cons Grid

A pros and cons grid lets you see at a glance which option is better and why. Pro is good; con is bad. Kiwi lists the good and bad points of each school.

Rio High School		Amazon High School	
Pros	**Cons**	**Pros**	**Cons**
Great soccer team (last year's national team champion)		Great soccer team (last year's national runner-up)	
Special program for foreign students; many English-speaking students			All Brazilian students; no program for foreign students
In Rio, near beaches			Far from Rio (2+ hours by train)
Cheaper ($3,000 a year)			Expensive ($5,000 a year)

Rio has four pros and zero cons; Amazon has one pro and three cons. "Rio High School is the place for me!" Kiwi thinks. She stays up until 4:00 a.m. filling out the online application.

Second Thoughts

The next day, Kiwi's watching the evening sports news on ESPN. Something a commentator says about the Yankees grabs her attention.

"Why can't the Yankees win despite all their superstar players?" he asks. "Think about all the players who never become starters because the owner decides to hire ready-made superstars from other teams. The rookies have it the worst. How can they develop their talent if they never get to play? On a strong team, sometimes new players never get the chance to develop into great players. It's no wonder the team's morale is so low."

The commentator has a point. Did Kiwi look at all the right information when she made her choice about schools in Brazil?

Kiwi goes back and thinks about her goals. "My goal isn't to play for the best soccer team," she realizes. "I want to become the best player I can be, by putting myself in the best soccer environment. And I want to learn a second language and get to know a new culture."

Kiwi realizes that her pros-and-cons chart might not have given her the right answer. She needs to think this through again.

Problem-Solving Toolbox: Evaluation Chart

An evaluation chart can be more detailed than a simple list of pros and cons. It can help you weigh how good each good point is, how bad each bad point is, and how important each one is to you.

To start off, Kiwi makes a list of all the things she wants in a new school. Then she ranks the importance of each point: high, medium, or low. She gives each school up to five plus marks.

What Do I Want in a School?	How Important Is This?	Rio High School	Amazon High School
Great environment to improve at soccer	High	?	?
Great place to learn a new culture and language	Medium	?	?
Cost (must be no more than $3,000 a year)	High	+ + + ($3,000 a year)	+ ($5,000 a year)
Close to Rio de Janeiro	?	+ + + + + (in Rio)	+ (2 hours away)

As Kiwi looks at her chart, she begins to ask herself some new questions:

▶ "What makes a great soccer environment for me?"

▶ "How good is Rio's program for foreign students, really? If there are lots of foreign students, how much will I learn about Brazil?"

▶ "Could I get a scholarship so that Amazon's tuition would be closer to $3,000?"

▶ "Is it that important to be close to Rio?"

Kiwi needs more information to fill out her chart completely. She makes an action plan and writes down a list. Now she knows what she's got to do next.

Questions	Actions to Take
1) What really makes a great soccer environment for me?	• Ask Coach Jones what he thinks is most important for a great soccer environment.
2) Is Rio's program for foreign students that strong? Is it a good idea to go somewhere with lots of U.S. students?	• E-mail Rio High's admissions office and ask to write to a few of the foreign students there.
3) Could I find a scholarship?	• Contact Rio and Amazon and see if scholarships are available. • Look for scholarships from the government or the U.S. Soccer Federation.

Finding a Great Soccer Environment

The next morning Kiwi calls Coach Jones and asks for his advice. "What really makes a good soccer environment?" she asks.

Coach Jones tells her, "The most important thing for you is to be surrounded by great players that you play with and compete against every single day." He says that she needs to get as much playing time as possible. And he warns her that some teams tend to bench their second- and third-string players, and only let the first string play. Kiwi should look for a school where all the players get on the field as much as possible. And the quality of the coaching matters too.

"Which school is better, Rio or Amazon?" Kiwi asks. But Coach Jones says he doesn't know. He has a friend, though, who coaches soccer in Brazil, and he offers to have this coach call Kiwi.

Coach Jones's friend, Coach Zico, calls Kiwi that very night. He tells her that he agrees with Coach Jones about what makes a great soccer environment. And of the two schools, he recommends Amazon. "Rio is famous for only letting their starting lineup play games," he tells her. "But Amazon lets all their players play in an equal number of games." And he thinks that

Amazon has better coaching than Rio. "Rio's known for their celebrity coaches," Coach Zico explains. "But they coach the adult national team too, so they're not at the school that much. Amazon's coaches spend a lot of time with their players. They're not famous, but that doesn't mean they're not good."

Now Kiwi can make a new evaluation chart for "Great soccer environment." She assigns Rio and Amazon plus marks for each of the three categories that make up a great soccer environment. Then she gives each "high importance" plus mark three points. "Medium importance" plus marks get two points, and low ones get one point. So Rio gets 25 points out of a possible 40, and Amazon gets 40 out of 40.

What Do I Want in a School?		How Important Is This?	Rio High School	Amazon High School
Great environment to improve at soccer		High	?	?
	How good my teammates are	High	+ + + + + (great, championship team)	+ + + + + (great, runner-up team)
	Chance to play many games	High	+ + (only first-string players get to play)	+ + + + + (all strings get to play)
	How good the coaches are	Medium	+ + (celebrity coaches but not much face time)	+ + + + + (great coaches, a lot of face time)
		Overall rating	25	40

Learning a New Language and Culture

Now Kiwi needs to compare the two schools to see which would be a better choice for helping her learn Portuguese and about Brazil's culture.

She gets in touch with Rio and asks if she can contact three American students already at the school. Here's what the first one e-mails her:

"The program for foreign students here is really helpful. They teach classes at a slower pace. But we speak a lot of English, so we don't learn that much Portuguese."

The second student complains about how many American students there are at the school. "There are more than thirty American students here, and we all take classes together and hang out after school. We don't mix with the local students that much. Sometimes I feel like I'm still in the U.S."

The third student feels the same way. "I don't have any real local friends," she writes. "If you really want to experience the culture here and learn the language, you should go to a school that only has local students. That's how you'll learn."

Now Kiwi can make a new chart for "Learning a new language

and culture." She figures out points the same way she did for the "Great soccer environment" chart. Rio ends up with 11 points out of a possible 20, and Amazon gets 16 out of 20. Amazon High School is looking better and better.

What Do I Want in a School?		How Important Is This?	Rio High School	Amazon High School
Great place to learn a new language and a new culture		Medium	?	?
	Spending lots of time with locals	High	+ + (30+ U.S. students)	+ + + + + (All Brazilian students)
	Special program for foreign students	Low	+ + + + + (Available, good program)	+ (Not available)
Overall rating			11	16

But it's still more expensive than Rio. What can Kiwi do about the high tuition?

Finding Tuition

First Kiwi tries to find a scholarship. But Amazon High doesn't offer any to foreign students. There are some scholarships from the government, but the deadlines to apply for these have already passed.

Kiwi begins to feel really down. It looks like she might have to go to Rio after all—even though she's decided that Amazon would definitely be the best school for her.

After practice that Saturday, Coach Jones pulls Kiwi aside. "How'd your talk with Coach Zico go?" he asks.

Kiwi tells Coach Jones everything—how great Coach Zico had been, how much he'd helped her, how she really wanted to go to Amazon now, except . . .

"Except what?" asks Coach Jones.

"My family can't afford the tuition," Kiwi says sadly.

"Really?" said Coach Jones. "That's too bad. You know, there

are a lot of soccer foundations that give scholarships. Did you check out any of those?"

"I didn't know about that!" Kiwi exclaimed. She couldn't wait to get home and start surfing the web.

Coach Jones was right. Kiwi found three soccer foundations that offered scholarships to high school students. She applied to all three, got one, and when fall came, she was on her way to Amazon!

Shaping Your Life by Challenging Your Decisions

Kiwi challenged her own decisions and took action to change her life. She not only has a talent for soccer, but she worked hard over the years to develop her skills. It didn't hurt that she's a nice person, too; that made the people around her go out of their way to help her. We can learn several lessons from Kiwi:

▶ Spend less time worrying about what's wrong, and more time thinking about what actions you can take to achieve your goals. And then take those actions!

▶ Ask for advice. You don't have to figure everything out on your own.

▶ Challenge your own thinking process and your own conclusions. Ask these questions:

- What are the pros and cons?
- Am I thinking about all of them?
- Which choice looks best if I consider all of the pros and cons, not just some?
- Are these pros really pros?
- Are these cons really cons?
- Are there things I could do that would make the pros even better or get rid of the cons altogether?

▶ Am I thinking about the right points to make this decision? How important is each point?

▶ Is my evaluation correct? Am I using the best, most accurate, most up-to-date information I can get?

Problem solving is easy when you know how to set a clear goal, figure out how to reach it, put your plan into action, and review your progress and make changes to your plan as you go.

If you make problem solving a habit, you'll be able to make the most of your talents and take control of your life. You can solve not only your own problems, but the problems of your school, your neighborhood, your city—and maybe even the world.

Acknowledgments

I WOULD LIKE to thank my family, friends, mentors, classmates, teachers, colleagues at McKinsey from all over the globe, the publishing staff of the original Japanese book and of the English edition in the U.S., the illustrators, my agent, and the Delta Studio staff for all the support you have provided, for everything you have taught me, and for making this journey so precious and exciting. I would like to visit each one of you to thank you personally in the upcoming month.

I would like to also send my special thanks to the former office manager at McKinsey, Tokyo, Masao Hirano; my editor Catherine Frank; the illustrator Elwood Smith; and the Delta Studio staff, Seita Yui and Takashi Yamashita. Masao was very supportive of my educational initiatives and provided me with the opportunity to write *Problem Solving 101*. Catherine has done so much to make *No Problem!* suitable for children. Elwood has added so much charm to the book with his wonderful drawings. Seita and Takashi has supported me so much to make this journey so fun, heart-warming, and exciting.